THE MIDLIFE MOVEMENT
8 Steps to a Happy & Healthy Lifestyle
For Women of a Certain Age
by
Mary Boyer
Master Trainer, Fitness Design Specialist
Lifestyle Coach and Nutrition Therapist

THE MIDLIFE MOVEMENT
8 Steps to a Happy & Healthy Lifestyle
For Women of a Certain Age
by
Mary Boyer
Master Trainer, Fitness Design Specialist
Lifestyle Coach and Nutrition Therapist

Copyright 2017 Mary Boyer /Photos Julie Vessell (Distinct Photography)
This work is licensed under a Creative Commons. Attribution-Noncommercial-No Derivative Works 3.0 Unported License. Attribution — You must attribute the work in the manner specified by the author or licensor (but not in any way that suggests that they endorse you or your use of the work). Noncommercial — You may not use this work for commercial purposes. No Derivative Works — You may not alter, transform, or build upon this work.

Disclaimer: The information contained herein is not intended to be a substitute for professional medical advice, diagnosis, or treatment in any manner. Always seek the advice of your physician or other qualified health provider with any questions you may have regarding any medical condition. All information contained in this book, including but not limited to text, graphics, images, information, third party information and/or advice, food, recipes, exercises, menus, psychology, websites, links, including but not limited to any content by employees, consultants, or writers and contributors, and or any other material contained herein are for informational and educational purposes only and is not intended to replace or override any information provided by a physician. Before starting this or any nutrition and exercise program, seek the advice and approval of a qualified physician first. By reading this book, the reader does hereby acknowledge that it is their sole responsibility to review this Disclaimer and any other disclaimer or waiver included in the book.

EPUB ISBN
Library of Congress Control Number:

INTRODUCTION

I had an epiphany, an *aha* moment as Oprah says, in the Fall of 2011, while parked in front of the government assistance building. Like the seventy percent of single, divorced mothers entering middle age and starting over, I contemplated this "card" as a means to making my life easier. The struggle was real, and for those of you reading this, you can understand the tug of war going on inside my head. As I sat there yelling at God, wondering why he hadn't shown up to fix this mess, I caught a glimpse of myself in the rearview mirror and what it revealed was horrifying. Through all the self loathing, pity parties, and toxic relationships going on, I pictured my girls and the cards they were dealt, and thought, "Is this really the person I want to be, the one they'll aspire to be? Do I want them to pity me like they do their dad? Do I want to enable them to become weak and depend on others to make it through life?"

I put that car in reverse so fast and hightailed it home with clarity of what I must change in order to prove to myself and my children that women, at any point in their lives, can start over, with nothing, and reinvent themselves. This was a defining moment of motherhood for me, empowering me to teach my offspring to become self sufficient, independent, and in control over what life threw their way.

If you are experiencing a similar situation, it can be a defining moment for you, too.

As I drove home, I started to formulate a plan, an outline of how I would never ever have to contemplate applying for that card or staying at poverty level. This *aha* moment also shed light on the unhealthy vices I had acquired in the last few years, binge drinking and playing Russian roulette with my weight, abusing my body through over training, and living a generally unhealthy life, both mentally and physically.

My story is not entirely unique, but it's mine, and I'm here to share with you how I turned it around and became everything I envisioned. Through reinvention and a little intervention, I've become what I set out to be—a successful entrepreneur in the fitness industry who motivates hundreds of clients to healthier and happier lives. And now I'm an author. I am healthy and happy, internally and externally, but that's not the most important thing. What matters most is that my girls respect me and consider me a role model, an example of who'd they'd like to become, and that trumps any title. It wasn't easy but, then again, nothing in life worth having comes easy, right?

This book is my roadmap for my success, and it can be yours, too. Attitude is everything, so reflect on and follow these steps and I promise you'll have a renew sense of clarity, direction, and vision for what your life can become. You'll create a personal commitment, resilience, and wisdom to get you to those goals over the long haul. You'll implement a holistic regiment of health habits to align your physical and emotional transformation while implementing tools to build connection and support with others on your journey.

You are Your Lifestyle

There's an attitude that comes with success; it's powerful, it's ruthless, and it acts with conviction, yet only one percent of us create it and use it. Why is that? For most, the power of a positive attitude carries a tremendous burden. There's an overwhelming feeling of having to portray a positive attitude every day and, should you falter, holy shit, it'll rain rivers of sarcasm and snark from those around you. Like it or not, there are those who relish in the excitement of those who fail. When others fail, it makes them feel better about their failures, too. The importance of a positive, healthy attitude never crossed my mind until my life crumbled around me.

I believe a multitude of things we've done throughout our lives shapes and determines who we are. Our past, the choices we've made, our relationships, and our attitude, behaviors, and habits are the outline of who we are. We won't know our full description until we take our last breath. The book of our life, in essence, won't be complete until we take our last breath.

We are given life and an imperfect biological

makeup, and then set free to become something of our choosing. I believe we are all destined for greatness, but it is our responsibility to fulfill that destiny.

Attitude is Everything

Believe it or not, we have control over most things. Many of us, though, deny this and become award-winning complainers and victims. Although our circumstances are legitimate and valid—the dissolution of marriage, for example—our attitude determines our actions and how we handle things. Whether we're wrong or right, who wants to admit their faults? Not me! Who wants to check their attitude? It's so easy to say, "I never saw it coming."

My Story

More than seventy percent of middle-aged women with children end up divorced and starting over, and it is that commonality I share with many. I share the fear, hatred, lost faith and trust, a lust for life, love, and, yes, sex. I share the tears, the pity parties, vulnerable moments, excessive mood swings, and bottles of wine lined up on the kitchen counter alongside a bag of M&M's. I've had and have been the toxic friend, family member, and parent.

I've been there, and I dug my way out of it. I'm

proof that you can go from wanting to bury someone's balls in the middle of the Vegas desert to walking arm in arm with him at your daughter's wedding.

It happened to me. I saw something coming, something that ultimately ended my marriage. The red flags surrounded me. Lack of communication and major trust issues and the evil necessity, money.

My story isn't entirely unique: I'm a divorced mother of three who didn't want to live paycheck-to-paycheck. I'm not suggesting I had it worse than others, but my story is mine, and no matter the situation, we all feel the immense angst and trepidation of negative life changes.

At forty, I realized the days of denying the end of my marriage and the reality of my finances were over. I wasn't living the dream, and that comfy, cozy suburban life I pretended to live was about to end.

As the details emerged, and the death of my marriage hit home, for the first time in eighteen years I felt truly alone; as hard as that was, I was okay with it because I was primed and ready for the change. I was about to formulate a plan to become completely self-sufficient and happy.

I was willing and excited to make the changes, but I was a newly single, forty-year-old mother whose financial situation easily qualified for government assistance. The good news was that I was done depending on anyone or anything to survive. The better news was that I was determined to be successful.

I prayed my stubbornness, work ethic, and willpower would keep me from falling victim to playing the "mishandled and abused" card. Don't get me wrong; I often felt that way and wanted to most of the time. I struggled week after week, budgeting the new life for my kids and me on a salary equivalent to poverty.

Fortunately, I've had nine years of growth in my personal, spiritual, and professional life, and still continue to grow every day. During those years I've had several defining, 'ah hah' moments alongside the "I want to punch myself" ones.

I've learned life lessons and moved forward, focused on being the best Mary I can be, and now it's my turn to help others to do the same.

If I can inspire and empower someone to release the same toxicity and work on themselves, I will have received the best payment. It's not easy; we women love to complain, stir up drama, and justify our lives and situations with a semi-truck full of excuses. It's time to stop. It's time to take back our lives and be the best versions of ourselves we can be—the ones we were meant to be.

I'm still guarded, and though I haven't forgotten what happened, I don't waste energy on it. I won't lie; the hardest thing to do is forgive, but it's the first step to finding peace and taking back your emotional power. Unfortunately, it doesn't happen overnight.

What worked for me might not work for you. You might have to tweak it a touch to make it work, but that's okay. I'm not here to dictate how you derive your independence from self-loathing. I'm here to tell you my story and motivate you to write your own.

One Step Forward, Two Steps Back

For me, patience was a must for my journey, but it was also the positive trait I lacked the most. The problem with the positive traits we lack is that, in an effort for us to gain them, the universe often smacks us in the face with them. When you put something out there, karma, the universe, God, whatever you choose to call it, sends it your way. When I finally hit my rock bottom, I knew that if I wanted to love again, laugh out loud, and move on, I'd have to be patient and allow myself the opportunity to learn and grow.

If that sounds like I sat around and waited to be better, that's not the case. I did the hard work and, believe me, it was hard.

A New Me, A New Career

Newly single and no longer required to be my ex-husband's cheerleader, turning 40 was like seeing the pot of gold at the end of the rainbow. I was ready for the next step—building a fitness and lifestyle coaching business. The goal was to have my company built by word of mouth, reputation, and a touch of advertising. I finally had a direction and a purpose.

I'd been a hair stylist and a mother, both of which I considered to be careers that shaped and transformed people. Wasn't that what a mother did, transform her babies into functional adults? And, certainly, a hair stylist transformed people, too. Who doesn't feel fabulous after having a fantastic new hairstyle? I did what was necessary to move forward and create a better life for myself, but the truth was, I really wasn't.

With each passing day, I found it incredibly difficult to resist battling my disastrous life with toxic conversations— ones I knew were harmful and fueled with hate. They helped validate and make me feel complacent, at least for the moment. I also found comfort in two polar opposite, yet equally addictive forms of recreation: drinking and exercising. I was the biggest hypocrite, yet I insisted I was in control of both. One made me forget and feel the obliviousness of denial, and the other gave me a sense of control over something—my body.

I simply wasn't ready to practice the vomit I preached as a certified lifestyle coach and fitness trainer.

That was my hell; I was entitled to my feelings, so why not surround myself with those who could identify, right? That's what you do to make yourself look and feel better; you seek out the individuals who'll amplify your messed up state of mind.

The Internal & External Cleansing

Nothing sucks more than to see your reflection of whom you've become staring back at you from the mirror. It shows every flaw, every scar, right down to the abuse you put on yourself. It reflects all your emotions; it's unforgiving, leaving you vulnerable and naked. For me, that reflection was my wake up call.

As I stepped out of the shower early one morning after washing away the evidence of a wine induced, groggy sleep, I stood in front of the mirror as I usually did getting ready for work. But that time I hesitated long enough to catch a true glimpse, and what I saw was the face of an imposter. I remember thinking, who is that? Where did that soft, flawless Mary Kay skin go? And my hair, I prided myself on having great hair, had thinned so much I could have been the poster child for Rogaine! My body, my once prized possession, was gone, too.

It wasn't pretty. In fact, it was terrifying.

I knew that day I needed to make changes, but the only way out was to come clean. I had to be one hundred percent honest with myself about my life choices, my habits, and my denial. I needed to own all of it and take responsibility. I couldn't live like that anymore. My divorce didn't define me, but I'd let it, and it was time to forgive—both my ex-husband and myself—and move on.

After two years of self-entitled negativity, hangovers, and unhealthy friendships, I finally decided to take the bull by the horns and get well. I practiced what I preached. I lived the lifestyle I told my clients would transform them and give them a path to a happy, healthy, fulfilling life.

And I had been right all along. Everything I'd taught my clients worked. I continued to focus on educating myself on fitness, nutrition, and lifestyle coaching. I became a sponge, soaking up every bit of new information I could because I knew it would continue to transform both my clients and me.

The changes in me were evident. The woman who once feared nothing more than speaking in front of a group of people wouldn't shut up. I told everyone not only my goals and what I'd been doing, but also what I planned to do and how I could help them. I came out of my shell, little by little, like that scared turtle picked up on the side of the road, and finally I held my head up, proud, for all to see.

My confidence and self-esteem improved, and aesthetically my body transformed. The gift of good genes and an athletic build aside, my newfound knowledge of heath and wellness gave me a better understanding of physiology and the power of good food. Because of that, my training intensified. I no longer ran miles and miles but incorporated strong, intense and quick functional movements into a solid fitness routine focused on both the mind and body. Of course, I'm still human, and I still made mistakes, and even though I knew what to do, I didn't always do it. I was in a much better place than I'd been before, though, and that is called progress.

Peeling Back the Layers

I like to think of my changes as an onion. For me, the onion signifies my metamorphosis—with every layer peeled representing an opportunity to reconstruct my behavior and attitude and get rid of a few vices. Boy, did I need an adjustment! For starters, I had to acknowledge the rotting aroma of my current situation, deal with the inevitable burn and tears of that pain and loss, and move towards tears of and laughter and healing as I embarked on this voyage.

Those first outer layers rough to peel. They pulled away slowly, stubborn and resistant to my efforts. Each piece shed was fragile and vulnerable, almost like a newborn baby. Looking back, I consider those early layers a rebirth of sorts.

As hard as it was, those were the first few steps in my true transformation; it was time, and those close to me knew it, too. They saw through my rough and tough exterior, and wanted me to resolve all the negative and hateful emotions and stop beating myself up over what was. And as much as I wanted that, too, I constantly battled the bitter, grudge-carrying divorcee residing in me.

I wanted to relinquish that Mary and live the healthy lifestyle I taught others, but just as there are more than a few layers to every onion, I'd only just begun peeling away mine.

While I adjusted my attitude, I also took stock of the people in my life and the things I valued. Something was missing, and that something was spiritual guidance.

I was raised a Catholic, thanks in part for my New York-raised Irish mother. I spent many Sundays and holidays sitting uncomfortably in church pews, occupying myself with thoughts of gymnastics and friends, counting people wearing glasses, or designing new hairstyles for every head in my view. I was there in body, but not in spirit.

That foundation did teach me about faith, but what I needed for this layer to come off wasn't so much faith as it was guidance. I needed a therapy of sorts to guide me through the process of peeling the layer that would ultimately heal my soul.

I ordered books online and read each one I could about people who'd come from hard times or tragic lives and made something of themselves. I was particularly drawn to stories of those who had dug themselves from the bowels of tragedy and found happiness inside.

The first book I read was Life Without Limits: Inspiration for a Ridiculously Good Life, the story of Nick Vujicic, an Australian Christian evangelist born without completely formed limbs. His story made mine look like a Disney movie! The man was born without limbs, contemplated suicide and dealt with circumstances I couldn't even begin to imagine, and I was wallowing in circumstantial, changeable self-pity because my life hadn't turned out like I'd planned.

I needed to read his story. I needed to know that there were hundreds, thousands of others in the world whose lives were worse than mine, but who triumphed over their adversity and came out better. I needed the motivation of others' success to pull me out of my funk.

I refused to let another year be lost to an unhealthy attitude. Subconsciously, I knew I could do better. I knew I could feel better and rise above my issues. My reputation defined me as the queen of having a positive, fearless, never quit attitude. Even though I'd spent many months faking it, or being "this close" to owning it, I'd yet reached the place where I felt whole, complete, and happy from within. Nick Vujicic's story helped me start my journaling process, a definite necessity of changing for the better. At first, my writings were like a distracted, hyperactive, third grader who hit the door running when the teacher said "recess," but that didn't matter. The point was to get my feelings on paper as both a release and as a way to determine patterns in my thought processes, my life, and my emotions that needed to change. I wrote to heal.

One evening while the girls slept, my old dog and I sat in my bed and wrote an outline, a checklist of sorts of what I needed to do to launch a brand new me. I wanted to redefine my view and society's view of mid-life for a newly single woman, and I was determined to make it happen.

The next book I read was Joel Osteen's <u>Daily Readings from It's Your Time: 90 Devotions for Activating Your Faith, Achieving Your Dreams, and Increasing in God's Favor</u>. His book offered the same theory as the first I'd read: life will challenge us with hardship and roadblocks. I loved the 90 days worth of devotional excerpts. I needed to wake up each morning to a motivating and inspiring message that encouraged happy, healthy thoughts instead of wanting to beat my ex to a pulp.

You know how it is when you offer the best researched and on point advice to your child and it goes in one ear and out the other? Then along comes someone else, saying the same thing and suddenly, the child gets it? For me, that parent was God, and I wasn't listening. Instead, I listened to the critics who offered every opinion under the sun when I expressed my thoughts on the subject of faith. I ignored the critics and spent the next 90 mornings reading that book, and still today it provides words of encouragement through Scriptures and prayer without the pressure to conform.

The third book, the Bible, arrived by way of a neighbor friend who ultimately became a client. She had faith, belief, and communication with the one source I denied and rebelled against. I had the strength and willpower of a not-so-well-received fallen angel. Together, we were a hot mess, but little did I know that our conversations would serve me well along my journey.

I decided to read one chapter in the book of Proverbs a day, and spent my time in the car in conversation with God. Most of the time I yelled at him, playing the "blame him because I'm the victim" game, and I never felt him carry the weight in his part of the conversation.

Like everything in life, we want the quick fix, the fast results. God didn't plop down next to me and tell me what to do, so I gave up. It was my mess, and I'd fix it on my own, because asking for help was only for the weak, and that wasn't me.

Even though I'd all but given up on God, I felt a tug toward my friend and the conversations we'd had. She had a way of reaching out at the time when I needed her most, each time bringing her Bible and using it in our talks. This woman, a client of my life coaching business, was coaching me, and we both knew it. It was easier to advise others and help them exchange poor choices for healthier ones, but to address my own was a nightmare.

The tsunami called my life picked up speed, and I wanted to run to the safety and security of my parents, to go back to my childhood even. I wanted to feel the comforts of unconditional love, knowing that my life would end up fine. I was a complete contradiction. I wanted to be strong and show others I was fine, but inside I was nothing but a scared little girl.

As I peeled away at the onion layers, I saw things I hadn't noticed before. That old saying about friendships being only for a season is true. People come into our lives when we have a particular need to fill and, if we're lucky, some of them become real, honest-to-goodness friends. Others leave, and that's okay. There are even honest-to-goodness friends that leave, too. It's the way it works.

I saw friends who weren't real friends, and I realized that sometimes letting go is best. I needed compassion and love, friends that would stand by me in all my craziness. Those who didn't, I needed to bid adios. Time is valuable and wasting it with those who are ill equipped to be what we need is pointless.

Not to long ago someone said to me, "Don't deny yourself a relationship based on your past experiences; it's not fair to that person." It was frighteningly true. My marriage wasn't the fairytale I'd hoped for. Ultimately, it disappointed my parents, who'd grown to think of my ex as their child. It also disappointed my children, who saw that "forever" wasn't forever, and when it wasn't, mom spent most of her time working, leaving them living with their grandparents full-time. I wasn't happy with the image I'd given my girls, but my meager income wouldn't support us and I had to work to pay the bills.

The work, the bitterness, and the lack of a happy ending made me fearful of ever having something special with a man again. I just didn't want it. But there were times—times when I'd let my mind wander to the possibilities of whoever the guy of the moment was—and then fear would take over and I would bolt. It wasn't fair, but regaining trust in people and in love itself is a slow journey, and I was already in the midst of one life-altering journey; two would have been brutal.

What I Did to Get My Groove Back
The 8 Steps to a Happy & Healthy Life

Changing our lives isn't easy, and neither is taking responsibility for our actions and choices we've made. It takes work—brutal, emotionally demanding work. The good news is you're completely capable if you have two things—desire and motivation. Without those two things, nothing in your life will ever change.

Attitude is everything, and your mindset will make or break you. If there's one thing I encourage you to start working on, it's having a positive attitude. Even when you're faced with difficult situations, remain positive. The world today thrives on limits, excuses, living an average lifestyle, and staying comfortable in a fixed mindset—basically, resisting change, and not working to improve yourself. If you're already engrossed in this, it's time to pull yourself out. Do you have the desire to change? Are you motivated to make it happen? Half-ass attempts are not acceptable; you must be fully invested for this to work. Are you ready? Then let's go.

Step One
Define What You Want

We've been conditioned to believe wealth and success come by way of inheritance, the chosen few who sucked up, or those with rare talent. We've justified this and avoided setting substantial goals and having big dreams for fear of failure; we've created that fixed mindset. Many are conditioned to act and work in an environment that's safe and enables their behaviors. This ultimately creates dependency and a complacent attitude.

What do you want? Think about that. What do you really want, not hope for or dream of? What do you value internally? Money? Love? Time? Freedom? Define your goal.

Whatever you want, whether it's happiness, independence, cash in your pocket, or a brand new house, it doesn't matter. The steps are the same. We women in the midst of life changes have to focus on ourselves first. You are the center of not only your life but your children's lives, too. If you're not happy, no one is happy. So define what will make you happy.

Take that goal and keep it with you everywhere you go. Write it down on sticky notes and put it in your car, your purse, on your fridge, closet door, bathroom mirror, wherever you can see it. Live and breathe that goal.

I feared setting goals—defining them and writing a plan of action—for fear of failure. I had this crazy idea in my head that my plan would be graded, so I remained average, letting fear once again hold me back from my future successes.

Ultimately, I had to get out of my own way, put fear in its place, and write with conviction. I had to accept the possibilities of setbacks and defeat and not let them distract me. Once I did this, I had the power and freedom to outline and plan my goals with confidence.

Step Two
Plan, Plan and Then, Plan Some More

To start my business, I needed to educate myself, find clients, and market myself. Whatever it is you want to start, begin by creating a plan, setting daily, weekly and monthly goals that represent and define what it is you're in pursuit of and how you'll become successful. Check them off, one by one as you go, and don't forget to reward yourself when you reach them. In a healthy way, of course.

The checklist is super important! I remember thinking, "I don't need a 'list;' I got this stored in my head. Wrong!! The list, like your goals, can change and that's okay. Keep writing them down and checking off every little piece of work you conquer. Your action steps are what will make it happen. My suggestion is to keep a notebook handy and keep your plans and to do list with you at all times. I've tried to create these in Google docs, but I've found I'm more accountable when I actually write them with pen and paper.

I've struggled at times with certain tasks, feeling as though the steps I took didn't lead me to my final destination. I had to remind myself that patience and maintaining a positive outlook were necessary, and failing didn't mean failure—it was simply part of the process. Nothing worth having comes easily, and nothing ever happens overnight.

Step Three
You Can't Do it Alone, So Don't Try

I hated asking for help and find most woman

feel that way, too. We fear we'll appear stupid, so we internalize all things and then use and often abuse playing the victim—ultimately falling back to the security of our old vices. Women hate showing weakness, usually because we are judgmental and men simply can't understand enough to help us. If you're anything like me, you won't be able to do this alone. If you've played the victim or been submissive, allowing someone else to determine what you wanted and how you felt, it's time to take action and not sit around and wait or hope for it.

But how?

Find a mentor, a friend, a family member, a professional. Choose someone you admire, someone living a life you respect. Allow them to advise and help you reach your goals.

Be coachable; be willing to make mistakes and learn from them without jumping on the defensive. Expect to be criticized; how you handle that feedback will set you apart from the rest of the world and allow you to be all you can.

When I finally realized the amount of time I wasted not asking for help and allowed schooling in the areas I was weak, things started to come together and success and opportunity arrived.

    I decided to embrace other females who are leaders and entrepreneurs living the lifestyle I wanted, instead of shying away, feeling inadequate, and playing victim to whatever the circumstances were in the moment. This change in attitude set me free to become everything I wanted and to do it with confidence. It's amazing what happens when you can sit with people who've been there and brainstorm without judgment. It's a mindset; turn off caring about what others think and get busy. I also changed my attitude about going at things alone and realized the value of the saying, "There's strength in numbers." Let's stick together, ladies; let's empower each other and learn from one another while holding each other up—you know, like a good bra.

    Women should empower women. We should be picking each other up, not stabbing each other in the back. We should be opening more lines of positive communication, being true friends, and using that old business theory of constructive criticism to help each other.

Step Four
Write Down Your Thoughts, Hopes, Dreams, EVERYTHING

Determining what you want and creating a plan to get it is just the beginning. Journaling should be your first step but, unfortunately, many of us don't realize we should journal until we've already figured out something is missing.

Journaling will help you define your goal more clearly, and, yes, it might change what you choose what you seek. If it does, that's okay. This isn't a written in stone, be-all-or-end-all thing. It's your life. Journaling may help you realize the things you thought you wanted aren't what you want. It will also help you determine your steps, the process, and what you need to do to heal your heart, mind, and body.

Step Five
Do What has to be Done

Success should never be treated as an option or left for someone else.

It's going to be hard. You're going to want to quit. Don't.

Do the work. Take the risks. Cry the tears. Be tired. Be frustrated. Be scared.

Most of all, be motivated and keep an open mind to allow yourself to move forward. If you have a vision and believe from the depths of your soul that the one thing you're completely passionate about has an opportunity to make a difference, then take the risk. Become obsessed with the details, like a kid trying to stay inside the lines in a coloring book. Stay focused and don't quit. We need to channel that obsessive behavior toward our goals.

Fortunately for me, I was raised in a household where having a "never give up" work ethic was important, and saying "I can't" was frowned upon. I could obsess easily over the things I was good at, staying focused and driven to accomplish my goals, but when it came to stepping out of my comfort zone, forget about it! Getting uncomfortable raised the percentage of failure, so I played it safe. Lesson learned again: fearing the unknown and not stepping outside the box was going to hold me back from reaching my goals and living the life I desired. Not only is it important to recruit people to help you along the way, but read or listen to books having to do with your goals and passion. One that I refer to often and to others is Grant Cardone's <u>The 10 X Rule</u>. I love his backstory, and the decision he made to get obsessed in making every goal happen by putting in the time, effort, and action steps necessary to dominate without ego. Success is your duty, obligation, and responsibility. His book offers so much more in how to get what you want by not being afraid to go big. Several goal setting books tell you to set small, realistic, obtainable ones that are measurable. Grant says, hell no, set goals that are unrealistic, not obtainable and one hundred percent over the top! By doing so, you'll end up getting further along then if you went small and played it safe.

Step Six
Patience is a Virtue, so Practice it

We are all works in progress, and it will take some longer than others to achieve their goal— that's okay. I'm still working on mine because as I grow, my goals change. I add to them; I remove from them. You'll do the same.

You'll have days where you'll want to give up and wallow in self-pity, days that will frustrate you and send you over the edge. Be prepared for those and push through them.

Understand that change doesn't happen overnight. You're creating something new, big, and exciting, so give it time. Don't let impatience rule your emotions.

Step Seven
Eat, Sleep, Workout, Repeat

I hear people apologize for so many things, including being happy. They're afraid to show their happiness because it might offend or hurt someone else. That's completely absurd.

Yes, this book is about focusing on you, your goals, your happiness, and your success, but to find true happiness you have to be well, emotionally and physically. If your body isn't well, your mind ultimately can't be either. You must eat well, exercise, work toward eliminating stress, and take care of yourself. Have you gone to the doctor lately? When was your last physical? Get it done. Make sure your health is attended to, and do what you can to be healthy physically.

Take it from someone who continued to learn the hard way. Being healthy is a state of mind. You must be willing to prioritize yourself and at the same time sacrifice something to gain a healthier mind/body.

Step Eight
Forgive, Forget, and Move On

The process of becoming whole, finding your inner peace, and being the best you can be is about you and only you. Don't let anyone else rule it, run it, or determine its value. Don't do it for revenge, to show someone you're better than they thought, or for any other reason than because you want to do it for yourself because you deserve to be happy.

So there you go! It doesn't seem too hard, but

be prepared. It might be. You'll have to work hard every single day to make these eight steps work for you. Remember, this is your life, your plan, and your future. Edit as you must; don't be afraid to make changes, to be changed.

I know it's not easy to ask for help—that was a huge fault of mine—but suck it up and put your pride aside. Be willing to reach out to those you trust and those whose success matches what you're shooting for. As I said earlier, it's vital to be in a healthy place physically and mentally to achieve success. Feeding the body and brain healthy fats, carbs, and protein five to six times a day and getting 30 minutes of activity that includes cardiovascular movement, strength, and mobility will increase your good endorphins. Schedule your training at minimum three times a week, stay disciplined, and value your health—no one else will.

CONCLUSION

Reflecting back to the beginning of my book, I wrote that there's a multitude of things we've done throughout our lives that have shaped us. The choices we've made in relationships, our attitudes, behaviors, and the habits we've formed are the outline of who we are; we won't know our full description until we take our last breath. One of the key lessons I've learned while writing this book is that my past does not define me. I can't go back and change any of it, so I must apply the lessons learned from the choices I made and continue to build my foundation. Now more than ever I realize this foundation I'm building comes with many layers, and each one of those layers is a representation of me. With that, I no longer judge or limit myself from getting to the next level. As I exit my 40's (with pride, I might add) and anticipation of what the 50's hold, I have a better understanding of who I am and what my purpose is. As I reflect back on this decade and the day I stood alone in my kitchen in the house that I was about to lose, fearing the unknown with a defeated attitude, I realize I was living in the moment, and all that mattered was getting through the days and wasting a lot of time on hate and revenge. I was restricting myself from growth by using my circumstances as excuses instead of learning devices. Had I been open to the power of reflection and the importance of communication, support, and establishing a plan, I could have been happier and healthier a lot sooner. Then again, this is life; you must take the good with the bad and hope you learn a lesson or two.

It took this whole decade for me to believe I'm destined for greatness, and for that to happen it had to start with my attitude and me. I said it earlier and live by it now: attitude is everything. It's my responsibility to fulfill my destiny. There's no more hoping or wishing for a better life, relationships, love, happiness or success; there's no more sabotaging with excuses and talking myself down or out of it. I I want it bad enough there has to be a plan—a positive mindset, no matter the obstacles. In the end, these layers will build me up or they'll bring me down; it's my choice. I've also learned the value of patience. Let me clarify. I'm still working on this, but patience is no longer my foe but my friend.

The pursuit of defining who I am meant evaluating every relationship and situation that occurred—good or bad—and learning from the outcome. Some left marks of inspiration, motivation, and laughter, while several furthered my education in life and business; there were also disappointments and a few who broke my heart. I've had moments of serendipity and others by choice; in the end, all who showed up helped get me to where I am now.

Throughout this decade, I've fine-tuned the skill of listening. In the past, I spent more time reacting to situations and passing judgment than listening completely. The very reactive, emotionally-driven Mary back then has come full circle.

Emotions are a part of life but need not apply in certain areas. A personal trainer and lifestyle coach career, if allowed, can be very emotional and draining mentally. I allowed that, and it took its toll on my life. I now manage it very carefully with a tough love approach that encourages and empowers my clients to utilize tools such as reflection, journaling, creating an outline for their goals, cleaning up environmental stresses, and nutrition. I encourage the building of a healthy support team around them. I no longer cringe at the thought of laying it on the line, giving my honest opinion about whatever the issue is. If it's not received well, its okay. Life goes on.

I don't waste time on the little things, especially ones that I can't control. Let me tell you, that's been hard. As a certified control freak, this is where patience has lent a helping hand. Having support in my corner has allowed me the opportunity to move on, no longer dwelling on situations or people who aren't ready to grow.

At 49, life's good. I have a fabulous support team, a thriving business, and have met my match, my true love. The saying, "Living the dream," rolls off most people's tongue sarcastically, but not mine. I *am* living the dream—my dream—it's what gets me out of bed at 3:30 in the morning. It gives me the opportunity to share my passions and my education, never once feeling like I'm at a JOB. Recently, I watched a TED Talk from Simon Sinek, entitled "How Great Leaders Inspire Action." His message provided a powerful model for leadership, starting with the golden circle. In the center of this circle sits the question, "*Why?*" Why do you do what you do? He further explains a true leader should inspire others to do better and be better by setting the tone and being driven by goals and a purpose, not the end result. Too often many concern themselves with rank or command, losing sight of the bigger picture.

Watching this TED Talk confirmed for me that I'm on the right path in business and also in my personal life. I've never placed much importance on rank, or degrees, for that matter, though I don't discount them because I know they are valid. I know many people with less education who followed their passion and have gone further in life because of that passion. I'm not talking just financially either. When I say they've gone further, I mean emotionally, too. They are complete and happy.

Like I said earlier, my story may not be totally unique or even as unpleasant as some of yours, but I own the exclusive rights to my book and its content. Every chapter represents a layer of my personal makeup, my foundation, and until I take my last breath, I'm still under construction, still a work in progress.

I'm excited for you to start applying these eight steps. Remember, this is your plan, so take the time to define it. Do your due diligence, create a checklist, and journal everything. Be patient; it's yours to change if needed—nothing worth having happens overnight. Keep your inner circle full of positive people you can turn to for advice and boost your energy and spirit. Burn the midnight oil and obsess over your mission, but make sure to take care of you—no one else will.

In strength & for the love of embracing midlife, Mary

Being happy & healthy and having a successful career should always be an option.

ACKNOWLEDGMENTS

As I was growing up, I remember saying, "I'll never be like my parents or say the things they say." Famous last words. I'm the apple that didn't fall far from the tree. For all the moments I resisted your wisdom and advice and was defiant when you were just trying to protect me, I get it now and words can't express how much I appreciate you, love you, Mom and Dad. Never one time did you judge me or the choices I was making, but stood by my side and offered help where needed. Your grandkids and I will be forever grateful for helping me raise them to be strong, healthy and respectful human beings.

My three beautifully, talented daughters, what a ride this has been. Many times I wanted to hit the "do over" button, but in the end I realized, like you are now seeing as adults, that life is not all unicorns and rainbows. We must build character and take the good with bad in order to deliver a positive outcome if we want to succeed in this life. All I want is to be your hero and leave a legacy you'll be proud of. I love you.

Scott and Melissa, thank you for your honesty and love over the years. As much as it hurt sometimes to hear the truth, it's what was needed and it only made me stronger. I love you.

Staci, we are two peas in pod when it comes to our passion and our love for our careers. I thank you for giving me that extra boost of confidence back in 2005 to get my schooling in the health and fitness industry and to meet Dr. Jack, who became a significant part of my training. You were also the only friend who encouraged and empowered me at my lowest point, pre- and post-divorce, to see myself as a sexy and strong woman, not just physically but internally. Thank you, and may we continue to drink wine and laugh—love you.

Laurie and Doreen, best friends through thick and thin, and over 30 years of memories that I cherish. Laurie, you and your family comforted me in trying times and never once judged me. You've welcomed me with open arms, bottles of wine, and loads of laughter, and I'm grateful for our sisterhood. Love you to the moon and back.

Regina, in the midst of my divorce when life was crumbling around me, I finally found you, my long lost bestie from grade school. I know we are miles apart, but knowing you're safe and only a phone call away makes my life that much richer. Love you.

Lisa, you know me better than I know myself, and I love you for that. You have this way of articulating all things that go on in my head and my world and making sense of it all. Everything I went through in the last 10 years you've been part of, and never once did you leave my side; thank you for being my biggest fan. I love you.

A big shout to all the clients I've had the pleasure of working with over the years. You've inspired me and taught me so many valuable lessons—thank you.

Carolyn, who would of thought, years later after high school, we'd become friends and you'd edit my first book? You are amazing at this writing thing, and I look forward to many more collaborations. Thank you for your patience and time. Love you, lady.

Dave, my legit Viking, here we are in the midst of so many amazing things going on in our professional lives who would of thought we'd fall in love? The love and gratitude I have for you is beyond words. I have met my match, my soul mate and best friend. Day after day your words of wisdom in business and life have inspired me to do better and be better, wanting to reach levels I thought were impossible, I love you. Together we are a force to be reckon with. Go on now, git it!

ABOUT THE AUTHOR

Mary is a Master fitness trainer, lifestyle coach and nutritional therapist who's expertise in the field of health and fitness has helped hundreds of people unveil their full potential. Her formula provides personalized training along with nutritional guidance designed to create a mind - body connection.

Mary's mission with The Mid life movement is to reverse societies definition of how middle age should look, act and participate in life.

Be on the look out for future books, blogs and podcast relating to these topics.

For more information, you may contact Mary at: www.mary@trufitnesstribe.com

Visit her blog at: <ins>midlifemovement.wordpress.com</ins>

Made in the USA
Lexington, KY
28 June 2018